WILD FLOWERS

This I-SPY book belongs to:_____

Introduction

You can find beautiful wild flowers growing almost everywhere. But did you know that the first flowering plants appeared on our planet some 200 million years ago? Not all plants produce flowers but as flowering plants are so adaptable to different conditions, they are now the most successful plants on Earth. Ultimately, all animal life depends upon plants for its survival: they provide the food you eat and the air you breathe.

We depend on plants in other ways, too. Many medicines were originally obtained from plants, and some still are. The tall spikes of Foxgloves produce a drug called digitalis which is used in treating human heart conditions. And even the well-known aspirin was originally made from the Willow tree. So plants are not just beautiful; they are a vital part of all life on Earth.

Wild flowers grow in gardens, waste places, parks, hedgerows, along roadsides, in and around farmland, and on walls; some even manage to survive in the tiny strips of earth that form between paving slabs on a pavement. And there are others that you can look out for when you go to the seaside, pay a visit to a local wood, or go on holiday to wilder parts.

As more and more countryside is built upon, some wild flowers have fewer areas in which to grow. So when you go out into the country, remember a simple rule: 'Take only photographs! Leave only footprints'. This means that you shouldn't pick wild flowers even if they seem to be common. Just photograph them or make sketches or paintings. And don't leave your rubbish behind; it not only spoils the look of the countryside, it can be dangerous to animals and plant life.

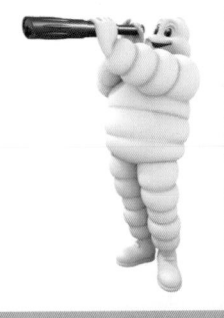

How to use your I-SPY book

The wild flowers in this book are arranged according to the usual colour of their. blooms, but the colours of flowers may vary quite a lot. So look carefully at the plants and don't be fooled if the colours of the ones you spot are a little different from those in the photographs. You need 1000 points to send off for your I-Spy certificate (see page 64) but that is not too difficult because there are masses of points in every book. As you make each I-Spy, write your score in the box and, where there is a question, double your score if you can answer it. Check your answer against the correct one on page 63.

WOOD ANEMONE

Scientific name
Anemone nemorosa

When does it flower?
March-May

Where is it found?
Open woods and hedges

What does it look like? About 6-30 cm (2-12 in) tall with white flower sometimes tinged pink

I-SPY points: 15

Date: _____

WHITE WATER-LILY

Scientific name Nymphaea alba

When does it flower?
June-September

Where is it found?
Lakes and ponds

What does it look like?
Floating leaves with large, decorative flowers

I-SPY points: 15

Date: _____

3

WILD STRAWBERRY

Scientific name Fragaria vesca

When does it flower? April-July

Where is it found?
Woods and shady roadsides

What does it look like?
Sprawling stems with long runners

I-SPY points: 15

Date: _____

WOODRUFF

Scientific name
Galium odoratum

When does it flower?
April-June

Where is it found? In woods

What does it look like?
Has bright green leaves edged with
tiny prickles

I-SPY points: 25

Date: _____

WHITE CLOVER

Scientific name
Trifolium repens

When does it flower?
June-September

Where is it found?
Open grassy places

What does it look like? Low
stems with three leaves

I-SPY points: 10

Date: _____

COMMON SCURVYGRASS

Scientific name
Cochlearia officinalis

When does it flower?
April-August

Where is it found? Sea cliffs and
along salted roadsides

What does it look like? Lots of
smooth, fleshy heart-shaped leaves

I-SPY points: 20

Date: _____

GARLIC MUSTARD

I-SPY points: 15

Double with answer

Date: _____

Scientific name
Alliaria petiolata

When does it flower?
April-July

Where is it found?
Open woods and hedges

What does it look like?
Tall, hairy stems with crinkled leaves which smell of garlic when handled

Do you know any other names for this plant?

WILD RADISH

Scientific name
Raphanus raphanistrum

When does it flower?
May-September

Where is it found?
Farmland and waste ground

What does it look like?
Tall with flowers that can vary in colour

I-SPY points: 15

Date: _____

6

WHITE CAMPION

Scientific name Silene latifolia

When does it flower?
June-September

Where is it found?
Dry fields and roadsides

What does it look like?
Tall with sweet-scented flowers

I-SPY points: 10

Date:_____

GREATER STITCHWORT

Scientific name
Stellaria holostea

When does it flower?
May-June

Where is it found?
Woods and hedgerows

What does it look like?
The tall flowering stems are four-sided and easily broken

I-SPY points: 10

Date:_____

COMMON CHICKWEED

Scientific name Stellaria media

When does it flower?
Throughout the year

Where is it found? Farms, gardens. roadsides, seashore

What does it look like?
Sprawling and leafy with small flowers

I-SPY points: 10

Date: _____

WOOD-SORREL

Scientific name
Oxalis acetosella

When does it flower?
April-June

Where is it found? Shady woods and hedgebanks

What does it look like?
Low-growing with leaves similar to clover

I-SPY points: 20

Date: _____

MEADOWSWEET

Scientific name
Filipendula ulmaria

When does it flower?
June-August

Where is it found? Damp
meadows, woods and ditches

What does it look like?
Tall, upright and leafy

I-SPY points: 20

Date: _____

ENCHANTER'S-NIGHTSHADE

Scientific name
Circaea lutetiana

When does it flower?
August-September

Where is it found?
Damp, shady woods

What does it look like?
Tall and single-stemmed with
tiny flowers

I-SPY points: 20

Date: _____

COW PARSLEY

Scientific name
Anthriscus sylvestris

When does it flower? May-June

Where is it found?
Woodland edges and roadsides

What does it look like?
Up to 1 m (over 3 ft) tall with branched flower heads containing many flowers arranged in an umbrella shape

I-SPY points: 5

Date: _____

WILD CARROT

Scientific name Daucus carota

When does it flower?
June-September

Where is it found? Chalky grasslands, especially near the sea

What does it look like?
Similar to Cow Parsley although the leaves are different

I-SPY points: 10

Date: _____

HEDGE BINDWEED

I-SPY points: 5

Date: _____

Scientific name
Calystegia sepium

When does It flower?
June-August

Where is it found? Hedges,
woodland edges and gardens

What does it look like?
Twining plant with large, funnel-
shaped flowers

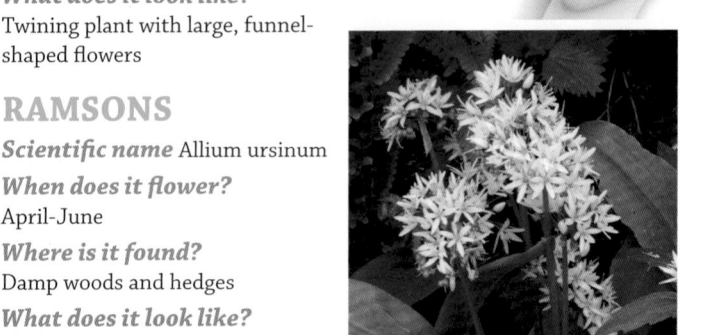

RAMSONS

Scientific name Allium ursinum

When does it flower?
April-June

Where is it found?
Damp woods and hedges

What does it look like?
Clusters of star shaped flowers,
and the whole plant smells
strongly of garlic so that it is often
called Wild Garlic or Wood Garlic

I-SPY points: 15

Date: _____

DAISY

Scientific name Bellis perennis

When does it flower?
Throughout the year

Where is it found?
Grassland including lawns

What does it look like?
A low plant with leaves arranged in a rosette

I-SPY points: 5

Date:

OXEYE DAISY

Scientific name
Leucanthemum vulgare

When does it flower?
May-September

Where is it found?
Most kinds of grassland

What does it look like?
Like a big daisy

I-SPY points: 10

Date:

GREATER PLANTAIN

Scientific name Plantago major

When does it flower?
May-October

Where is it found?
Fields, gardens and waste land

What does it look like?
A rosette of leaves from which the flower spikes rise up to 50 cm (20 in)

I-SPY points: 10

Date:

12

SUN SPURGE

Scientific name
Euphorbia helioscopa

When does it flower?
April-October

Where is it found? Fields, gardens and waste ground

What does it look like?
The 50 cm (20 in) stem ends in an umbrella-shaped flower head

I-SPY points: 20

Date: _____

WHITE DEAD-NETTLE

Scientific name Lamium album

When does it flower?
May-August

Where is it found?
Roadsides, wasteplaces, hedgerows

What does it look like?
Similar to the Common Nettle but with large white flower heads and no stinging hairs

I-SPY points: 10

Date: _____

I-SPY points: 50

Double with answer

Date: _____

COMMON NETTLE

Scientific name Urtica dioica

When does it flower?
June-September

Where is it found? Woods,
wasteplaces, hedgerows, gardens

What does it look like?
Tall, hairy plant with roughly
triangular, saw-edged leaves

*The young leaves are good
to eat – True or False?*

LORDS-AND-LADIES

Scientific name
Arum maculatum

When does it flower?
May-June

Where is it found?
Woodlands, hedgerows and ditches

What does it look like?
The flower spike is shrouded by a
leafy cowl

*What is the other well
known name for this
plant?*

I-SPY points: 15

Double with answer

Date: _____

COMMON POPPY

Scientific name Papaver rhoeas

When does it flower?
May-October

Where is it found? Farmland
and waste or disturbed ground

What does it look like?
The tall stems are bristly while
the leaves are toothed

I-SPY points: 10

Date:

RED CAMPION

Scientific name Silene dioica

When does it flower?
May-September

Where is it found?
Damp woods and hedgerows

What does it look like?
Similar to White Campion but red
and unscented

I-SPY points: 15

Date:

COMMON VALERIAN

Scientific name
Valeriana officinalis

When does it flower?
June-August

Where is it found?
Woods and roadsides

What does it look like?
Tall stems and tiny flowers in dense clusters

I-SPY points: 20

Date: _____

SCARLET PIMPERNEL

Scientific name
Anagallis arvensis

When does it flower?
May-October

Where is it found? Cultivated ground, roadsides and sand dunes

What does it look like?
Small, ground-hugging plant

I-SPY points: 20

Date: _____

BILBERRY

Scientific name
Vaccinium myrtillus

When does it flower?
April-June

Where is it found?
On heaths and moors and in woodlands on poor soils

What does it look like?
Thin woody stems with lots of bright green leaves

What colour are the edible fruits of the bilberry?

I-SPY points: 15
Double with answer
Date: _____

MUSK MALLOW

Scientific name Malva moschata

When does it flower?
July-August

Where is it found?
Open, dry grassy and bushy places, often on roadsides

What does it look like?
Hairy stems topped with clusters of big pink flowers

I-SPY points: 25
Date: _____

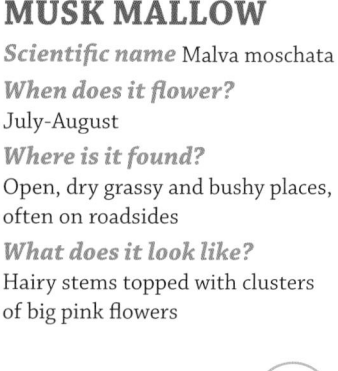

COMMON CENTAURY

Scientific name
Centaurium erythraea

When does it flower?
June-August

Where is it found?
All kinds of poor grassy places

What does it look like?
A basal rosette of pale green leaves hugs the ground

I-SPY points: 25

Date:_____

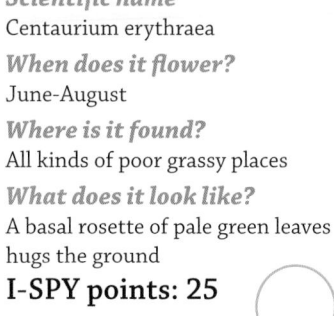

RAGGED-ROBIN

Scientific name
Lychnis flos-cuculi

When does it flower?
May-August

Where is it found?
Damp meadows and woods

What does it look like?
As its name suggests, the pink/red flowers have a ragged appearance

I-SPY points: 25

Date:_____

HERB-ROBERT

Scientific name
Geranium robertianum

When does it flower?
April-October

Where is it found?
Woods, hedgebanks, shingle
shores and on mountains

What does it look like?
About 40 cm (16 in) high with
hairy leaves and stalks

I-SPY points: 15

Date: _____

DOG-ROSE

Scientific name Rosa canina

When does it flower?
June-July

Where is it found?
Woods, hedges and scrubland

What does it look like?
The bushes bear flowers which are
white or tinged with pink

What are the fruits called?

I-SPY points: 10
Double with answer

Date: _____

HEMP AGRIMONY

Scientific name
Eupatorium cannabinum

When does it flower?
July-September

Where is it found? In damp
woods and on marshy roadsides

What does it look like?
Masses of tall stems topped by
dense pink flower-heads

I-SPY points: 20

Date: _____

CROSS-LEAVED HEATH

Scientific name Erica tetralix

When does it flower?
June-August

Where is it found?
In boggy heaths and moors

What does it look like?
Straggly, branching shrub with
many small (2-4 mm) leaves

I-SPY points: 20

Date: _____

THRIFT

Scientific name
Armeria maritima

When does it flower?
April-August

Where is it found?
Sea cliffs and salt marshes

What does it look like?
Groups of plants form mat-like clumps and the pink flowers are sweet smelling

I-SPY points: 20

Date: _____

REDSHANK

Scientific name
Persicaria maculosa

When does it flower?
June-August

Where is it found?
Roadsides, ditches, waste places and cornfields

What does it look like?
Has reddish stems and usually a dark blotch on each leaf

I-SPY points: 15

Date: _____

COMMON RESTHARROW

Scientific name Ononis repens

When does it flower?
July-September

Where is it found?
In dry grassy places

What does it look like?
Has a low, woody stem and small downy leaves

I-SPY points: 25

Date: _____

CREEPING THISTLE

Scientific name Cirsium arvense

When does it flower?
June-August

Where is it found? Fields, roadsides and waste places

What does it look like? Masses of prickly stems and leaves

I-SPY points: 10

Date: _____

BEE ORCHID

Scientific name Ophrys apifera

When does it flower? June-July

Where is it found? Mainly on chalk and limestone downland

What does it look like? Like a big furry bumble bee visiting a pink flower

BRAMBLE

Scientific name Rubus fruticosus

When does it flower? June-August

Where is it found? Woods, roadsides, bushy places, heaths and cliffs

What does it look like? Has very prickly, arching stems and pink or white flowers

What is the fruit of the bramble called?

I-SPY points: 50
Date:_____

I-SPY points: 15
Double with answer
Date:_____

RED VALERIAN

Scientific name
Centranthus ruber

When does it flower?
May-August

Where is it found? Cliffs,
quarries, walls and dry banks

What does it look like?
Grows in large tufts and has
smooth, oval leaves and red, pink
or white flowers

I-SPY points: 25

Date: _____

FIELD BINDWEED

Scientific name
Convolvulus arvensis

When does it flower?
May-October

Where is it found? Farms,
gardens, roadsides and by railways

What does it look like?
A trailing or climbing plant with
funnel-shaped pinkish, reddish or
even white flowers

I-SPY points: 10

Date: _____

LOUSEWORT

Scientific name
Pedicularius sylvatica

When does it flower? April-July

Where is it found?
Bogs, damp woods, moors and heaths where the soil is acid

What does it look like?
Quite variable in height with double-lipped flowers

I-SPY points: 50

Date:_____

CUCKOOFLOWER

Scientific name
Cardamine pratensis

When does it flower?
April-June

Where is it found? Damp meadows, streamsides, ditches, roadsides and on mountains

What does it look like?
Flowerhead contains between 7 and 20 four-petalled flowers varying from white to pink

What is this plant's other common name?

I-SPY points: 15
Double with answer

Date:_____

COMMON MALLOW

Scientific name Malva sylvestris

When does it flower?
May-October

Where is it found?
Roadsides, meadows, woodland

What does it look like?
The plant can reach heights of
1.5 m (5 ft)

RED CLOVER

Scientific name
Trifolium pratense

When does it flower?
May-October

Where is it found? Grassland

What does it look like?
It may be upright or sprawling
with three-leaved stems

I-SPY points: 15

Date: _____

I-SPY points: 15

Date: _____

SELFHEAL

Scientific name
Prunella vulgaris

When does it flower?
June-August

Where is it found? In grassy places and in open woods

What does it look like?
Oval pointed leaves on fairly short stems

I-SPY points: 15

Date:_____

TUFTED VETCH

Scientific name Vicia cracca

When does it flower?
June-August

Where is it found? Roadside hedges, field and woodland edges

What does it look like?
A showy, pea like plant which climbs using its tendrils

I-SPY points: 20

Date:_____

COMMON VETCH

Scientific name Vicia sativa

When does it flower?
April-September

Where is it found? Hedgerows,
woodland and field edges

What does it look like?
A pea like trailing or climbing plant
with down-covered stems

I-SPY points: 20

Date: _____

PURPLE-LOOSESTRIFE

Scientific name
Lythrum salicaria

When does it flower?
June-September

Where is it found?
Damp areas such as lake sides,
stream sides or fens

What does it look like?
Strong-growing spikes up to 1.5 m
(5 ft) tall

I-SPY points: 20

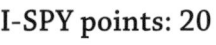

Date: _____

ROSEBAY WILLOWHERB

Scientific name
Chamerion angustifolium

When does it flower?
June-September

Where is it found? Waste places, rubbish tips, disturbed ground, cleared woodland

What does it look like? Strong-growing spikes up to 1.5 m (5 ft)

This plant is also called Fireweed; do you know why?

I-SPY points: 15
Double with answer

Date: _____

GREAT WILLOWHERB

Scientific name
Epilobium hirsutum

When does it flower?
July-September

Where is it found? Woodlands, stream banks, ditches and marshes

What does it look like? Bigger than Rosebay and with larger flowers at the top of the stem

I-SPY points: 15

Date: _____

29

HEATHER

Scientific name Calluna vulgaris

When does it flower?
July-October

Where is it found?
Heaths, moors, open woods and
boggy areas on acid soil

What does it look like?
A bushy, shrub-like plant with
spikes of small flowers

*It is also called Sling.
True or False?*

**I-SPY points: 10
Double with answer**

Date:_____

BELL HEATHER

Scientific name Erica cinerea

When does it flower?
May-September

Where is it found? On the drier
soils of acid heaths and moors

What does it look like?
The flowers are larger and more
bell-shaped than those of Heather

I-SPY points: 15

Date:_____

BITTERSWEET

Scientific name
Solanum dulcamara

When does it flower?
May-September

Where is it found?
Damp hedges, woodlands and river banks

What does it look like?
It is a weak growing, straggly plant which uses others for support

I-SPY points: 15

Date: _____

FOXGLOVE

Scientific name
Digitalis purpurea

When does it flower?
May-September

Where is it found?
Open woods, scrubland and hillsides on acid soils

What does it look like?
Tall, handsome spikes of thimble-shaped flowers

What organ of the human body is Digitalis used to treat?

I-SPY points: 15
Double with answer

Date: _____

STINKING IRIS

Scientific name Iris foetidissima

When does it flower? June

Where is it found? In woods and scrub and on sea cliffs

What does it look like? Thick tufts of evergreen leaves and bright orange seeds

I-SPY points: 50

Date: _____

GROUND-IVY

Scientific name
Glechoma hederacea

When does it flower?
March-June

Where is it found? Damp woods, hedges and waste ground

What does it look like? This ground trailing plant has kidney-shaped leaves and it forms carpets where it grows. The leaves smell strongly when crushed

I-SPY points: 15

Date: _____

COMMON DOG-VIOLET

Scientific name Viola riviniana

When does it flower?
April-June

Where is it found? Woods, roadside banks and grassy fields

What does it look like?
A low-growing plant with heart-shaped leaves

I-SPY points: 15

Date: _____

RED DEAD-NETTLE

Scientific name
Lamium purpureum

When does it flower?
March-November

Where is it found?
Waste land and cultivated ground

What does it look like?
Similar to other dead-nettles but with small, reddish-purple flowers

I-SPY points: 10

Date: _____

I-SPY points: 15

Date: _____

LESSER BURDOCK

Scientific name Arctium minus

When does it flower?
July-September

Where is it found?
Open woods, hedges, waste places

What does it look like?
A tall, bushy plant with heart-shaped leaves

WATER MINT

Scientific name
Mentha aquatica

When does it flower?
July-September

Where is it found? Bogs,
marshes, lake and stream sides

What does it look like?
Upright plant up to 80 cm (32 in),
smelling strongly of mint

I-SPY points: 15
Date: _____

SPEAR THISTLE

Scientific name Cirsium vulgare

When does it flower?
July-September

Where is it found? Grassy
places, by roads, waste ground

What does it look like?
Strong-growing plant with prickly
winged stems and spear-shaped
leaf prickles

I-SPY points: 15
Date: _____

GREEN ALKANET

Scientific name
Pentaglottis sempervirens

When does it flower?
April-August

Where is it found?
On roadsides near gardens

What does it look like?
Tall, rough stems with oval leaves

I-SPY points: 30

Date: _____

VIPER'S-BUGLOSS

Scientific name Echium vulgare

When does it flower?
May-September

Where is it found?
Chalk downs, shingles, dunes

What does it look like?
Tall, hairy plant with masses of
trumpet-shaped flowers

I-SPY points: 15

Date: _____

HEDGE WOUNDWORT

Scientific name
Stachys sylvatica

When does it flower?
June-October

Where is it found? Shady places such as woods and hedgebanks

What does it look like? Similar to a dead-nettle, with broad leaves

How does this plant get its name?

I-SPY points: 15
Double with answer

Date: _____

MARSH WOUNDWORT

Scientific name
Stachys palustris

When does it flower?
July-August

Where is it found? In marshy places and on damp roadsides

What does it look like?
Similar to Hedge Woundwort but with much narrower leaves and brighter flowers

I-SPY points: 30

Date: _____

MUSK THISTLE

Scientific name Carduus nutans

When does it flower?
June-August

Where is it found?
In grassy and bushy places

What does it look like?
Has spiny stems and big drooping flower-heads

I-SPY points: 30

Date: _____

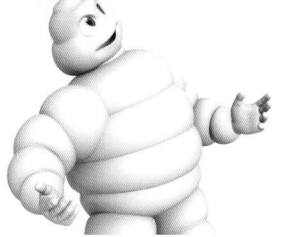

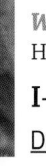

BETONY

Scientific name
Stachys officinalis

When does it flower?
June-August

Where is it found?
In open grassy and bushy places

What does it look like?
Has slightly hairy, oblong leaves

I-SPY points: 20

Date: _____

PYRAMIDAL ORCHID

Scientific name
Anacamptis pyramidalis

When does it flower?
July-August

Where is it found? In chalk grassland and on sand dunes

What does it look like?
The thin stems are topped by a dome-shaped mass of flowers

I-SPY points: 50

Date:_____

SOUTHERN MARSH-ORCHID

Scientific name
Dactylorhiza praetermissa

When does it flower?
June-July

Where is it found?
In open marshy places

What does it look like?
Has a stout stem and bright green shiny leaves, sometimes spotted

I-SPY points: 50

Date:_____

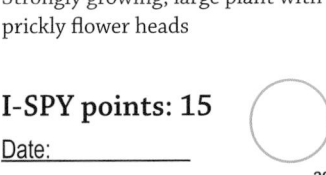

WILD THYME

Scientific name
Thymus polytrichus

When does it flower?
April-September

Where is it found?
Dry grassland, heaths, dunes

What does it look like?
Ground-hugging plant which
smells of the herb when crushed

I-SPY points: 25

Date: _____

WILD TEASEL

Scientific name
Dipsacus fullonum

When does it flower?
July-August

Where is it found? Waste places,
open woods, river banks

What does it look like?
Strongly growing, large plant with
prickly flower heads

I-SPY points: 15

Date: _____

BLACK HOREHOUND

Scientific name Ballota nigra

When does it flower?
June-August

Where is it found?
In hedgebanks and bushy places, often near houses

What does it look like?
A bushy, weedy plant with a strong unpleasant smell

I-SPY points: 30

Date: _____

EARLY-PURPLE ORCHID

Scientific name Orchis mascula

When does it flower?
April-June

Where is it found?
Chalky woods, downs and sea cliffs

What does it look like?
A typical orchid with the rosette of leaves spotted in a purplish colour

I-SPY points: 50

Date: _____

I-SPY points: 15
Double with answer

Date:

MEADOW CRANE'S-BILL

Scientific name
Geranium pratense

When does it flower?
May-August

Where is it found?
Roadsides, hedgerows, edges of grassy meadows

What does it look like?
Strongly growing plant with deeply divided leaves

How does the plant get its name?

SHEEP'S-BIT

Scientific name
Jasione montana

When does it flower? May-July

Where is it found? On acid soils, on heaths, moors, grassy roadsides, cliffs and shingle

What does it look like?
Fairly low, wiry stems topped with blue 'pom-pom' flower-heads

I-SPY points: 25

Date:

41

GERMANDER SPEEDWELL

Scientific name
Veronica chamaedrys

When does it flower?
April-July

Where is it found? Grassland, hedges, roadsides, open woodland

What does it look like?
The stems grow along the ground at first before reaching upwards

I-SPY points: 15

Date: _____

HEATH SPEEDWELL

Scientific name
Veronica officinalis

When does it flower?
May-August

Where is it found?
On grassy heaths and moors

What does it look like?
Creeping, hairy stems and leaves with erect flower-spikes

I-SPY points: 25

Date: _____

BUGLE

Scientific name Ajuga reptans

When does it flower?
May-June

Where is it found? Damp
grassland and woodland clearings

What does it look like?
The stems are hairy on two
opposite sides and the flowers
appear in rings around the stem

I-SPY points: 15

Date: _____

HAREBELL

Scientific name
Campanula rotundifolia

When does it flower?
August-September

Where is it found?
Dry, chalky grassland

What does it look like?
Nodding thin stalks, thin leaves
and bell-shaped flowers

I-SPY points: 15

Date: _____

CHICORY

Scientific name
Cichorium intybus

When does it flower?
June-September

Where is it found? Roadsides, grassy and waste places

What does it look like?
A rather straggling and stiff-stemmed plant.

If roasted and powdered, the roots are used as a substitute for coffee. True or False?

I-SPY points: 15
Double with answer

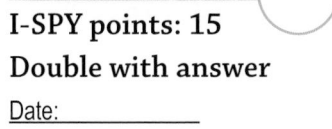

Date: _____

BLUEBELL

Scientific name
Hyacinthoides non-scripta

When does it flower?
April-June

Where is it found? Woodlands and other shady, damp places

What does it look like?
The leaves are narrow and shiny and surround the flower stem

I-SPY points: 15

Date: _____

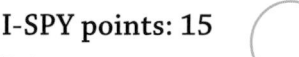

44

GREATER KNAPWEED

Scientific name
Centaurea scabiosa

When does it flower?
June-September

Where is it found? Dry
grassland, hedgebanks, roadsides

What does it look like?
Stiff, branched stems with deeply
cut leaves

COMMON KNAPWEED

Scientific name Centaurea nigra

When does it flower?
June-August

Where is it found?
In all kinds of grassy places

What does it look like? Stiff
upright stems with uncut leaves

I-SPY points: 10

Date: _____

I-SPY points: 15

Date: _____

MARSH-MARIGOLD

Scientific name Caltha palustris

When does it flower?
March-May

Where is it found? Marshes, ditches, the edges of water courses

What does it look like? Like a large buttercup with round leaves

I-SPY points: 15

Date: _____

CREEPING BUTTERCUP

Scientific name
Ranunculus repens

When does it flower?
April-September

Where is it found?
Damp meadows and roadsides

What does it look like?
The plant is tough, tall, hairy and has palm-like leaves

I-SPY points: 5

Date: _____

46

GREATER KNAPWEED

Scientific name
Centaurea scabiosa

When does it flower?
June-September

Where is it found? Dry
grassland, hedgebanks, roadsides

What does it look like?
Stiff, branched stems with deeply
cut leaves

COMMON KNAPWEED

Scientific name Centaurea nigra

When does it flower?
June-August

Where is it found?
In all kinds of grassy places

What does it look like? Stiff
upright stems with uncut leaves

I-SPY points: 10

Date:_____

I-SPY points: 15

Date:_____

MARSH-MARIGOLD

Scientific name Caltha palustris

When does it flower?
March-May

Where is it found? Marshes, ditches, the edges of water courses

What does it look like? Like a large buttercup with round leaves

I-SPY points: 15

Date:

CREEPING BUTTERCUP

Scientific name
Ranunculus repens

When does it flower?
April-September

Where is it found?
Damp meadows and roadsides

What does it look like?
The plant is tough, tall, hairy and has palm-like leaves

I-SPY points: 5

Date:

46

YELLOW WATER-LILY

Scientific name Nuphar lutea

When does it flower?
June-September

Where is it found? Lakes, ponds and slow-running streams

What does it look like?
The roundish leathery leaves float at the surface and the flowers are carried above them

I-SPY points: 15

Date:_____

WILD MIGNONETTE

Scientific name Reseda lutea

When does it flower?
June-September

Where is it found?
Disturbed and waste land

What does it look like?
The bristly stems carry spikes of pale yellow flowers

I-SPY points: 15

Date:_____

PERFORATE ST JOHN'S-WORT

Scientific name
Hypericum perforatum

When does it flower?
May-September

Where is it found?
Open woods, scrub, dry grassland

What does it look like? When held up to the light the leaves seem to be marked with pale spots

I-SPY points: 15

<u>Date:</u>

COMMON ROCK-ROSE

Scientific name
Helianthemum nummularium

When does it flower?
May-September

Where is it found?
Dry chalk grasslands

What does it look like?
The flower looks like a single yellow rose

I-SPY points: 15

<u>Date:</u>

KIDNEY VETCH

Scientific name
Anthyllis vulneraria

When does it flower?
April-September

Where is it found?
Dry grassland, dunes, sea cliffs

What does it look like?
The flowers are carried in round clusters at the top of the stem

I-SPY points: 15

Date: _____

AGRIMONY

Scientific name
Agrimonia eupatoria

When does it flower?
June-September

Where is it found?
Dry fields, roadsides, waste land

What does it look like?
Upright, sometimes reddish stems with saw-edged leaflets

I-SPY points: 15

Date: _____

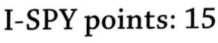

49

SILVERWEED

Scientific name
Potentilla anserina

When does it flower?
May-September

Where is it found? Damp fields,
hedgebanks, roadsides, waste land

What does it look like?
The leaves are arranged in rosettes
from which runners creep

I-SPY points: 15

Why is the plant so called? **Double with answer**

<u>Date:</u> _____

CREEPING CINQUEFOIL

Scientific name
Potentilla reptans

When does it flower?
May-September

Where is it found?
Dry roadsides and waste places

What does it look like?
A creeping, mat-forming plant
with long runners

I-SPY points: 25

<u>Date:</u> _____

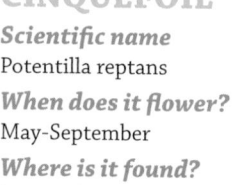

COWSLIP

Scientific name Primula veris

When does it flower?
April-May

Where is it found? Hedgebanks, roadsides, old meadows

What does it look like?
The rosette of Primrose-like leaves surround a medium-height flower stem

I-SPY points: 20

Date: _____

PRIMROSE

Scientific name:
Primula vulgaris

When does it flower?
March-May.

Where is it found? Woods and banks beside roads and railways.

What does it look like?
The flowers may be either pin-eyed (long style) or thrum-eyed (short style).

I-SPY points: 10

Score double for finding both kinds

Date: _____

YELLOW PIMPERNEL

Scientific name
Lysimachia nemorum

When does it flower? May-July

Where is it found?
In dampish woods

What does it look like?
Creeping stems in large masses

I-SPY points: 30

Date:

COMMON TOADFLAX

Scientific name Linaria vulgaris

When does it flower?
July-September

Where is it found?
Grassy and waste places

What does it look like? Like a
small-flowered garden snapdragon

I-SPY points: 10

Date:

52

CORN MARIGOLD

Scientific name
Chrysanthemum segetum

When does it flower?
May-August

Where is it found? In arable fields with wheat or other crops

What does it look like?
Masses of bright yellow flowers on tall stems

I-SPY points: 50

Date:

BULRUSH

Scientific name Typha latifolia

When does it flower?
June-August

Where is it found?
Beside rivers, lakes and ponds

What does it look like?
Long, stiff grey leaves and sausage-shaped flower-spikes

I-SPY points: 25

Date:

LESSER CELANDINE

Scientific name
Ranunculus ficaria

When does it flower?
March–May

Where is it found? Hedgerows, gardens, roadsides and woods

What does it look like?
A low-growing buttercup with heart-shaped leaves

I-SPY points: 10

Date:_____

GREAT MULLEIN

Scientific name
Verbascum thapsus

When does it flower?
June–August

Where is it found?
Dry grassy or stony places

What does it look like? It may reach 2 m (over 6 ft) in height; the leaves and stem are woolly

I-SPY points: 15

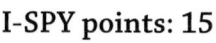
Date:_____

54

HONEYSUCKLE

Scientific name
Lonicera periclymenum

When does it flower?
June-October

Where is it found?
Woodlands and hedgerows

What does it look like?
A woody climbing plant with sweet-smelling flowers

I-SPY points: 15

Date: _____

SMOOTH HAWK'S-BEARD

Scientific name Crepis capillaris

When does it flower?
June-November

Where is it found?
Grasslands and waste places

What does it look like?
The flowers resemble small Dandelions carried on tall thin stems

I-SPY points: 10

Date: _____

55

COMMON RAGWORT

Scientific name
Senecio jacobaea

When does it flower?
May-October

Where is it found? Neglected fields, dunes and roadsides

What does it look like?
An upright, branched plant with strong-smelling leaves which are poisonous to livestock

I-SPY points: 5

Date: _____

TRAVELLER'S-JOY

Scientific name:
Clematis vitalba

When does it flower?
July-September

Where is it found?
In woods and hedgerows, mainly on chalk and limestone

What does it look like? A big woody climber with fragrant flowers

I-SPY points: 20

Date: _____

GOLDENROD

Scientific name
Solidago virgaurea

When does it flower?
July-October

Where is it found?
Dry woods, hedges, dunes, grassy
and rocky places

What does it look like?
The flowerhead takes the form of
a branched spike with many tiny
flowers

I-SPY points: 15

Date: _____

PERENNIAL SOW-THISTLE

Scientific name
Sonchus arvensis

When does it flower?
August-September

Where is it found? Gardens,
farms, roadsides, waste places

What does it look like?
Similar to the Dandelion

I-SPY points: 10

Date: _____

DANDELION

Scientific name
Taraxacum officinale

When does it flower?
Irregularly through the year

Where is it found?
Road verges, gardens, farmland, waste places, fields

What does it look like?
The flower stems are hollow and contain a milky juice

Where does the name come from?

I-SPY points: 5
Double with answer

Date: _____

CARLINE THISTLE

Scientific name Carlina vulgaris

When does it flower?
July-August

Where is it found?
In dry grassland

What does it look like?
Low-growing and prickly

I-SPY points: 35

Date: _____

GOLDEN SAMPHIRE

Scientific name
Inula crithmoides

When does it flower?
July-August

Where is it found?
On sea-cliffs and salt-marshes

What does it look like?
A big, fleshy-leaved daisy

I-SPY points: 50

Date:

COMMON FLEABANE

Scientific name
Pulicaria dysenterica

When does it flower?
July-September

Where is it found?
Ditches, marshy meadows and
damp roadsides

What does it look like?
A big, shaggy plant with masses of
yellow flowers

I-SPY points: 25

Date:

LADY'S BEDSTRAW

Scientific name Galium verum

When does it flower?
July-August

Where is it found?
In dry grassy places

What does it look like?
Masses of tiny, yellow flowers on sprawling stems

I-SPY points: 25

Date: _____

WOOD-SAGE

Scientific name
Teucrium scorodonia

When does it flower?
July-September

Where is it found?
Woodland edges, hedgebanks and other fairly dry places

What does it look like?
A downy plant about 30 cm (1 ft) high with wrinkled leaves

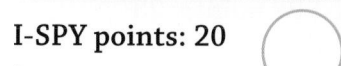

I-SPY points: 20

Date: _____

COLT'S-FOOT

Scientific name
Tussilago farfara

When does it flower?
February-April

Where is it found?
Waste land, dunes, river sides

What does it look like?
Dandelion-like flower but the
leaves are heart-shaped

I-SPY points: 20

Date: _____

YELLOW IRIS

Scientific name
Iris pseudacorus

When does it flower?
May-August

Where is it found? Ditches,
lakesides, river sides, wet woods

What does it look like?
Like a yellow garden iris

I-SPY points: 15

Date: _____

BROOM

Scientific name
Cytisus scoparius

When does it flower? May-June

Where is it found?
On dry acid soils such as heaths

What does it look like?
A small, dark green, spineless shrub

I-SPY points: 30

Date:_____

GORSE

Scientific name Ulex europaeus

When does; it flower?
March-June

Where is it found?
Heaths and hillsides

What does it look like?
A spiky bush

I-SPY points: 10

Date:_____

Index

First published by Michelin Maps and Guides 2009
© Michelin, Proprietaires-Editeurs 2009.
Michelin and the Michelin Man are registered
Trademarks of Michelin.
Created and produced by Blue Sky Publishing Limited.
All rights reserved. No part of this publication may be
reproduced, copied or transmitted in any form without
the prior consent of the publisher. Print services
by FingerPrint International Book production
- fingerprint@pandora.be
The publisher gratefully acknowledges the contribution
of the I-Spy team: Camilla Lovell and Ruth Neilson in
the production of this title.
The publisher gratefully acknowledges the contribution
of Premaphotos Wildlife who provided all the
photographs and the text in this I-Spy book.
Reprinted 2011   10 9 8 7 6 5 4

Answers: P6: Jack-by-the-Hedge, Jack-among-the-Hedgerow. **P14:** Cuckoo Pint. **P14:** True. **P17:** Black. **P19:** Hips. **P23:** Blackberry. **P25:** Lady's Smock. **P29:** Because it grows on burnt ground. **P30:** False. It is called Ling. **P31:** The heart. **P36:** Because the leaves were once used to dress wounds. **P41:** From the beak of the fruit which resembles a Crane's bill. **P44:** True. **P50:** Because the silky hairs make the underside of the leaves look silvery. **P58:** Dent de lion (lion's teeth) which refers to the toothed leaves

HOW TO GET YOUR I-SPY CERTIFICATE AND BADGE

Every time you score 1000 points or more in an I-Spy book, you can apply for a certificate

Here's what to do, step by step:

Certificate

- Ask an adult to check your score

- Ask his or her permission to apply for a certificate

- Apply online to www.ispymichelin.com

- Enter your name and address and the completed title

- We will send you back via e mail your certificate for the title

Badge

- Each I-Spy title has a cut out (page corner) token at the back of the book

- Collect five tokens from different I-Spy titles

- Put Second Class Stamps on two strong envelopes

- Write your own address on one envelope and put a £1 coin inside it (for protection). Fold, but do not seal the envelope, and place it inside the second envelope

- Write the following address on the second envelope, seal it carefully and post to:

I-Spy Books
Michelin Maps and Guides
Hannay House
39 Clarendon Road
Watford
WD17 1JA